WILDLIFE OF NORTH AMERICA

The Moose

by Annie Hemstock

Consultant:
Charles C. Schwartz
Wildlife Biologist
Alaska Department of Fish & Game

CAPSTONE
HIGH/LOW BOOKS
an imprint of Capstone Press
Mankato, Minnesota

Capstone High/Low Books are published by Capstone Press
818 North Willow Street • Mankato, Minnesota 56001
http://www.capstone-press.com

Library of Congress Cataloging-in-Publication Data
Hemstock, Annie.
  The moose/by Annie Hemstock.
  p. cm.—(Wildlife of North America)
  Includes bibliographical references (p. 45) and index.
  Summary: Details the characteristics, habitats, and life cycle of the largest
member of the deer family.
  ISBN 0-7368-0030-1
  1. Moose—Juvenile literature. [1. Moose.] I. Title. II. Series.
QL737.U55H465 1999
599.65'7—dc21
                                                                    98-3625
                                                                       CIP
                                                                        AC

Editorial Credits

Mark Drew, editor; Timothy Halldin, cover designer and illustrator;
  Sheri Gosewisch, photo researcher

Photo Credits

Borland Stock Photo/Charlie Borland, cover
Craig Brandt, 8, 11, 15, 16, 27
Dembinsky Photo Assoc. Inc./Claudia Adams, 6; Darrell Gulin, 18, 38; Carl R.
  Sams, 21; Mike Barlow, 36; Mark J. Thomas, 42–43; Doug Locke, 40
James H. Robinson, 35
Mark Raycroft, 22
Robin Brandt, 24, 29, 30, 32
Valan Photos/Michel Bourque, 19

Table of Contents

Fast Facts about Moose

Scientific Name: *Alces alces*

Length: Adult moose grow to be about nine feet (2.7 meters) long.

Height: Male moose are called bulls. Adult bulls measure about six feet (1.8 meters) tall from the ground to the shoulders. Female moose are called cows. Adult cows grow to be about five and one-half feet (1.7 meters) tall.

Weight: Adult bulls weigh 1,200 to 1,600 pounds (544 to 726 kilograms). Adult cows weigh 800 to 1,300 pounds (363 to 590 kilograms).

Physical Features: Moose have long heads, large bodies, long legs, and short tails. Moose may be golden brown to nearly black. Bulls have large spoon-shaped antlers with spikes on the edges. Bulls shed their antlers and grow a new set each year.

Habitat: Moose live in forests. They often live near rivers and shallow lakes.

Range: Moose live throughout Alaska and Canada. They live in some northern and western areas of the United States. Moose also live in the northern regions of Europe and Asia.

Behavior: Adult moose live by themselves. They sometimes live near other moose in areas where food is plentiful.

Food: Moose are herbivores. An herbivore is an animal that eats only plants. Moose mostly eat the leaves and twigs of trees and shrubs.

Reproduction: Bulls mate with cows sometime between late August and late October. Cows give birth between mid-May and early June. They usually have one or two calves each year.

Life Span: Moose live about 16 years.

State Symbol: The moose is Maine's state animal and one of Alaska's state animals.

Chapter 1

The Moose

Moose are the largest members of the deer family. The deer family includes elk, caribou, and white-tailed deer. All members of the deer family are mammals. A mammal is a warm-blooded animal with a backbone. The body temperature of a warm-blooded animal stays about the same despite the air temperature.

Moose live in the northern half of the world. About 500,000 moose lived in North America in 1950. Today, the moose population is about 1 million. Most North American moose live in Alaska and Canada. Others live in some parts of the northern and western United States.

Moose are the largest members of the deer family.

Long legs help moose travel through snow.

Physical Features

The moose is a large animal. It has a heavy body with long legs. Long legs help the moose travel through water and snow. The moose has hooves on the ends of its long legs.

The moose has a huge head and big ears. The moose's nose is long and droopy. A large flap of skin called a bell hangs from the moose's throat.

The moose's coat varies in color from golden brown to nearly black. Its coat may change color as the seasons change and as the moose ages. The moose gradually sheds its coat and grows a new one each summer and winter.

The moose's coat has two layers. The top layer is guard hair. Guard hair covers the moose's entire body. The moose's guard hair is thicker and longer in winter than it is in summer. This helps the moose stay warm and dry. Each guard hair is hollow and holds air. This helps the moose stay afloat in water when it swims.

Beneath the moose's guard hair is a layer of woolly fur. It covers the moose's body but not its legs and face. The fur provides extra warmth.

Bulls and Cows

Male moose are called bulls. Adult bulls stand about six feet (1.8 meters) tall at the shoulders. They weigh from 1,200 to 1,600 pounds (544 to 726 kilograms).

Adult bulls have two large spoon-shaped antlers with spikes on the edges. Bulls shed their antlers and grow a new set each year.

These sets of antlers are usually four to five feet (1.2 to 1.5 meters) across. Some bulls have sets of antlers that measure more than six feet (1.8 meters) across.

Female moose are called cows. Cows are smaller than bulls. They stand about five and one-half feet (1.7 meters) tall at their shoulders. They weigh 800 to 1,300 pounds (363 to 590 kilograms). Cows do not have antlers.

Behavior

Moose live alone for most of their lives. But they may live together in certain situations. Moose sometimes gather together in small groups during mating season. Cows live with their calves for about one year. A calf is a young moose. Moose also may live together in places where food is plentiful.

Moose communicate by making sounds. They roar like lions when they are upset. They snort when they are angry. Moose whine or moan when they are looking for other moose. Some moose sounds are so low that humans cannot hear them.

Cows are smaller than bulls. Cows do not have antlers.

O *Where Moose Live*

Moose also communicate with their bodies. The guard hairs on their necks and backs stand up when they are upset. Moose hold their heads low and flatten back their ears when they are angry. Moose also give off scents to send messages to other moose. They do this mostly during mating season.

Habitat
Most moose live in the forests that stretch across Canada and the northern United States.

Forests provide moose with food and good hiding places. Forests also provide shelter from snow during winter and heat during summer.

Moose often live near forest areas that have been cleared by fires, floods, or people. Many new trees and shrubs grow in these areas. Young trees and shrubs are good sources of food for moose.

Moose also live in wooded areas near streams, ponds, and lakes. They feed on plants that grow near the shore and in the water. Moose swim to cool off during the warm summer months. They also go into the water to escape insects.

Home Range

The area a moose occupies during its lifetime is its home range. The size of a home range varies with the season and the amount of food that is available. Most home ranges cover between five and 20 square miles (13 and 52 square kilometers). But some home ranges stretch across 100 square miles (259 square kilometers) or more.

Calves spend their first two years of life in their mothers' home ranges. Calves establish their own home ranges when they are about two years old.

Moose are not territorial animals. They do not protect their home ranges from other moose. Moose home ranges frequently overlap. This is so moose can find one another during mating season. Moose also need to find areas where food is plentiful. So they sometimes have to share good feeding sites.

Some moose have only one home range. Others have a summer home range and a winter home range. Moose with two home ranges migrate. Moose that migrate move from one range to another when the seasons change. Some moose migrate 80 miles (129 kilometers) to reach their summer or winter ranges. Calves learn migration routes from their mothers.

Moose prepare for mating season and winter in their summer ranges. They spend much of their time feeding. Moose migrate from their summer ranges when mating season begins or when snow becomes too deep.

Moose migrate from their summer home ranges when snow becomes too deep.

Chapter 2

Survival

Moose are watchful, careful animals. They have a strong sense of smell and sharp hearing. Moose use these senses to survive.

Moose use their strong sense of smell to find food and detect predators. A predator is an animal that hunts and eats other animals. Moose also use their strong sense of smell to find mates.

Large ears allow moose to hear even the slightest noise. Moose use their hearing to locate predators. Sharp hearing also helps moose communicate with one another.

Moose are watchful, careful animals. Their large ears allow them to hear even the slightest noise.

Moose eat by grasping food with their lips and tongues.

Feeding Habits

Moose spend most of the spring, summer, and fall eating. They must eat to put on large amounts of fat. Moose need fat to stay alive during winters when food is scarce. Fat also keeps them warm.

The foods moose eat vary with the seasons. Moose eat leaves and twigs during spring and summer. They also eat leafy plants that grow on land and in water. Moose eat twigs and branches during winter. They also eat tree bark.

Moose eat by grasping food with their lips and tongues. Moose have very limber lips. Their tongues are long and bendable. Moose clip the leaves and twigs with their front teeth. Moose then grind the food with their back teeth.

Moose swallow food without fully chewing it. They store it in their stomachs. Later, they spit up some cud. Cud is food that has been partly broken down. Moose then chew the cud thoroughly and swallow it again. This process helps moose break down foods such as branches or bark.

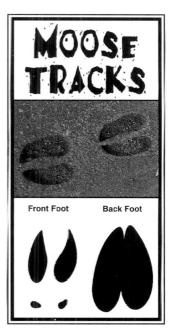

Predators

Adult moose have few predators. Bears, wolves, and people prey upon moose. Animal predators usually kill young, old, or sick moose. Predators sometimes kill cows that try to save their calves. People hunt moose for their meat and for their antlers.

Healthy moose often outrun predators. Moose can run up to 35 miles (56 kilometers) per hour. They sometimes fight off predators with their sharp hooves or antlers.

Moose often go into water to escape predators. Moose are strong swimmers. People have seen moose swim 12 miles (19 kilometers) without stopping.

Despite their size, moose are good at hiding from predators. They lie down in brush or tall grass. Their coloring allows moose to blend in with their surroundings.

Winter is the hardest season for moose to avoid predators. Moose are weaker during winter because food is scarce. Deep or ice-crusted snow makes it difficult for moose to outrun predators. Moose can travel easily in snow up to 28 inches (71 centimeters) deep. But they often become stuck in deeper snow because of their tremendous weight. Wolves are much

Moose are strong swimmers.

lighter than moose. Wolves often can travel on snow without becoming stuck.

Other Dangers

Moose face other dangers besides predators. Cars and trains frequently hit moose. Moose often travel on roads and railroads and feed at roadsides. This is especially true during winters when snow is very deep.

Parasites also are a danger to moose. A parasite is an animal or plant that needs to live on or inside another animal or plant to survive. One parasite that affects moose is a tiny worm that enters the moose's brain. Moose that have this parasite grow weak, cannot move, then die.

Moose often travel on roads and railroads and feed at roadsides.

Chapter 3

The Life Cycle

Moose prepare for their mating season in many ways. Bulls rub their antlers against bushes and small trees to scrape off the velvet. Velvet is the soft, furry skin that covers antlers while they grow. Velvet dies when antlers are fully grown. The antlers are white under the velvet. Blood from the velvet and juices from the plants that moose rub against color the antlers brown.

Cows move into mating areas shortly before mating season begins. Mating areas are usually near streams, lakes, or ponds. These places often have some open ground so cows can see bulls approach. Cows patrol their mating areas day

Bulls rub their antlers against bushes and small trees to scrape off the velvet.

and night. They also mark their areas with their urine. The scent helps to draw bulls near.

Sparring

Bulls begin to spar as mating season nears. These practice fights prepare bulls for battles with other bulls. Bulls may have to fight one another for cows during mating season.

Bulls first spar with trees. They push and scrape trees with their antlers. This allows bulls to learn the size, shape, and strength of their antlers.

Bulls also spar with each other. Two bulls lock antlers and push against each another. The bulls do not try to hurt each other. They spar to learn the other bull's strength. They also learn the size and shape of the other bull's antlers. This helps them understand their rank in relation to other bulls.

The Rut

The rut is another name for the mating season of the moose. The rut begins in late August and usually ends in late October. Cows mate

Bulls spar as mating season nears.

for the first time when they are between one and three years old. They must be in heat before they can mate. Cows that are in heat are ready to breed. Cows are in heat from one to 36 hours. They will be in heat again after about 25 days if they do not mate.

Bulls usually do not mate until they are at least five years old. Bulls that are actively mating stop eating for up to three weeks. Some bulls lose up to 20 percent of their body weight. They start eating again when the rut is over.

Moose search for and call to other moose during the rut. Cows make a moaning call to tell bulls that they are ready to breed. Bulls rattle their antlers against bushes and trees. They make a sound like a hiccup. Bulls whine and grunt to let cows know that they are near. Bulls also scrape the ground with their feet.

Bulls sometimes dig a shallow hole called a wallow. They then urinate in the wallow. Bulls often splash the muddy urine on their antlers. The scent of the urine draws cows.

Bulls rattle their antlers against trees and bushes to let cows know that they are near.

Bulls usually try to scare off their rivals before fighting.

Bull Fights

Bulls often fight one another for cows during
the rut. Younger and weaker bulls do not
challenge older, stronger bulls. Bulls of equal
strength fight. The bull that wins the fight
usually mates with the cow.

Bulls first try to scare off their rivals before fighting. They roll their eyes and lay back their ears. They gnash their teeth and grunt. They try to look bigger and stronger than other bulls.

Bulls fight if they cannot scare off their rivals. Deadly battles are rare. But bulls sometimes hurt each other during fights. Some bulls die from their wounds.

Birth

Cows go off on their own after mating. They leave their mating areas and return to their home ranges. Cows continue to eat to put on more fat for winter.

Cows begin looking for calving sites in spring. A calving site is a place where a cow gives birth. Cows look for calving sites that provide shelter and food. They often choose narrow strips of land near water. These sites help cows protect their calves from predators.

Moose calves are born between mid-May and early June. Calves weigh from 28 to 35 pounds (13 to 16 kilograms) at birth. Their coats are red-brown.

Cows younger than two years old usually give birth to one calf. Most adult cows have one or two calves. Some cows have three calves.

Calves

Calves can walk and follow their mothers within hours of birth. But they cannot walk steadily until they are about four days old.

Cows and calves are in constant contact for the first week. This helps them form strong bonds. After the first week, cows let their calves roam. But cows still stay close to their calves for up to three weeks.

Young calves drink milk from their mothers' bodies. The milk helps calves gain the weight they need to survive. Calves start eating solid food after about two months. But they continue to drink their mothers' milk until early fall. Calves usually weigh more than 300 pounds (136 kilograms) when they are five months old.

Calves stay with their mothers for one year. Cows teach calves many things during this time. They show calves how to avoid predators. They

Calves can walk and follow their mothers within hours of birth.

also teach calves migration routes. Cows chase their calves away when spring arrives. They do this to prepare for the birth of new calves.

Bulls and cows become adults at different ages. Bulls become adults at five years old. This is when they reach adult body size. Cows become adults at three years old.

Moose rarely live longer than 16 years. Their teeth wear down as they get older. This makes it hard for them to eat enough to survive.

Calves stay with their mothers for one year.

Chapter 4

Past and Future

Scientists believe that moose first appeared in Europe 500,000 years ago. They say moose migrated from Asia to North America 10,000 to 14,000 years ago. At that time, a strip of land connected the areas that are now Russia and Alaska.

Moose and Native Peoples

Native peoples in the northern parts of North America hunted moose for hundreds of years. Moose were a valuable source of food for these people. Many of them depended on moose meat for their survival.

Moose were a valuable source of food for native peoples.

Some native peoples had feasts when they killed moose. They believed moose gave their lives so that people might live. The native peoples gave thanks to the spirits of moose.

Native peoples used almost every part of the moose. They made clothing, beds, and tents from moose hides. Some native peoples made shields from dried moose skin. Others dyed moose hair and used it to decorate clothes and blankets. Native peoples also made tools from moose bones and antlers.

Moose also were part of the myths of many native peoples. The Abenaki (a-buh-NA-kee) people have a story that tells how the moose was created. The Abenaki are a group of Native American people. They live in southeastern Canada and the northeastern United States.

According to the myth, the creator made the moose very large. But the moose was too large for people to kill. So the creator decided to make the moose smaller. The creator squeezed the moose down to a smaller size. But the creator squeezed the moose unevenly. This is

Many native peoples have myths about moose.

Today, many people consider moose to be symbols of the wilderness.

why the moose has a long body, a humped back, and a large nose.

Moose and People Today

Moose are still important to people today. Many people consider moose to be symbols of the wilderness. Some people still hunt moose for their meat and their antlers. Other people enjoy watching moose in their natural surroundings.

Moose can be dangerous to people. Moose are especially dangerous during the rut and when cows are raising calves. Moose cause more human deaths in Alaska each year than bears do. Many of these deaths occur because people do not understand moose behavior.

Scientists are working to find out more about moose and their needs. They are learning about the ways in which humans affect moose. Forest and wildlife managers use this information to plan for the moose's future. They want to make sure that moose continue to flourish.

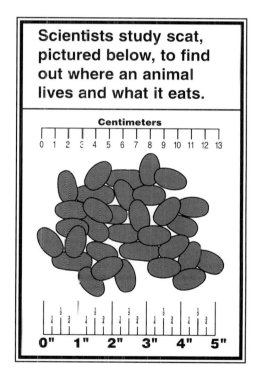

Scientists study scat, pictured below, to find out where an animal lives and what it eats.

Centimeters
0 1 2 3 4 5 6 7 8 9 10 11 12 13

0" 1" 2" 3" 4" 5"

Large Ears

Antlers

Droopy Nose

Bell

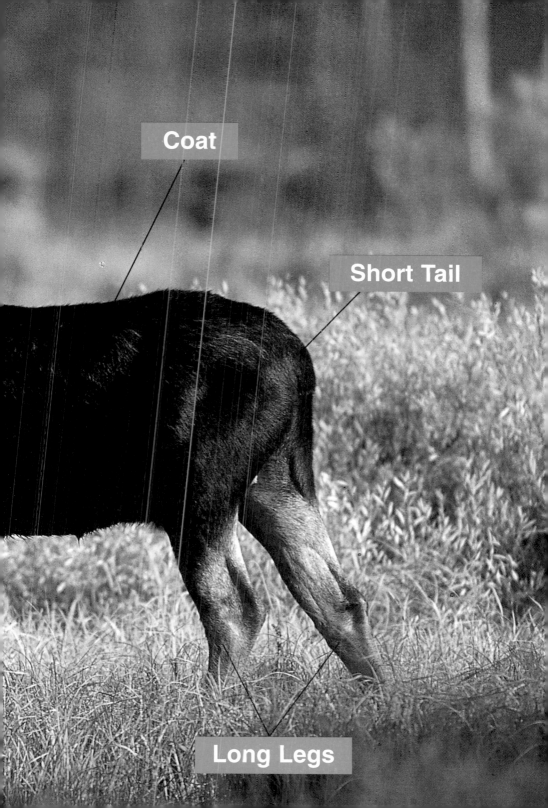

Coat

Short Tail

Long Legs

Words to Know

bell (BEL)—a large flap of skin that hangs from a moose's throat

communicate (kuh-MYOO-nuh-kate)—to send and receive messages

cud (KUHD)—food partly broken down in the stomach that is spit up and chewed again

herbivore (UR-buh-vor)—an animal that eats only plants

mammal (MAM-uhl)—a warm-blooded animal with a backbone

migrate (MY-grate)—to move from one place to another when seasons change

parasite (PAIR-uh-site)—an animal or plant that needs to live on or inside another animal or plant to survive

predator (PRED-uh-tur)—an animal that hunts and eats other animals

rut (RUHT)—the mating season for moose

spar (SPAR)—to practice fighting

velvet (VEL-vit)—the soft, furry skin that covers antlers while they grow

To Learn More

DuTemple, Lesley A. *Moose.* Early Bird Nature Books. Minneapolis: Lerner Publications, 1998.

Fair, Jeff. *Moose for Kids: Moose Are Like That.* Animals for Kids. Minocqua, Wis.: NorthWord Press, 1992.

Petersen, David. *Moose.* A New True Book. Chicago: Children's Press, 1994.

Ritchie, Rita and Jeff Fair. *The Wonder of Moose.* Animal Wonders. Milwaukee: Gareth Stevens Publishers, 1996.

Useful Addresses

Alaska Department of Fish and Game
Moose Research Center
34828 Kalifornsky Beach Road
Soldotna, AK 99669

Ministry of Natural Resources
435 James Street South
Suite 221
Thunder Bay, Ontario P7E 6S3
Canada

National Wildlife Federation
8925 Leesburg Pike
Vienna, VA 22184

Wildlife Management Institute
1101 14th Street NW
Suite 801
Washington, DC 20005

Internet Sites

Bering Land Bridge National Preserve: Moose

http://www.nps.gov/bela/html/moose.htm

Land of Adventure Alaska Wildlife Series: Moose

http://www.juneau.com/loa/HTML/moose.htm

The Magnificent Moose Project

http://www3.northstar.K12.ak.us/schools/awe/
moose/moosepage.html

Moose Page

http://www.halcyon.com/moose/welcome.html

Tracking and the Art of Seeing: Moose

http://www.grtblue.com/tracking/TrackingMoose
288.html

Index